I0410811

Wetlands

of

NEW JERSEY

UNITED STATES DEPARTMENT OF THE INTERIOR
FISH AND WILDLIFE SERVICE ~ OFFICE OF
RIVER BASIN STUDIES ~ REGION V ~ BOSTON MASS.

TABLE OF CONTENTS

APPENDICES

WETLANDS INVENTORY OF NEW JERSEY

1. <u>Purpose and Scope of Inventory</u>. - Concerned about the loss of wildlife habitat through the increased rate of wetland drainage, fill, and pollution, the Fish and Wildlife Service became committed to a program of integrated land-use planning wherein the wildlife use of wetlands fits into a plan including all other economic uses of these lands. As an early phase in the development of that program, a nation-wide inventory of wetlands resources was initiated by the Service. This New Jersey inventory is an integral part of that effort. Since allowable time limits do not permit a complete inventory at this time, it was agreed that, within each of the states, regions containing a minimum of 90 percent of the wetlands of importance to waterfowl should be dealt with first.

In New Jersey, those regions were delineated by L. G. MacNamara of the New Jersey Division of Fish and Game. In each selected region, areas identified by wetland symbols on U.S.G.S. maps and/or topographic maps prepared by the New Jersey Department of Conservation and Economic Development, and containing a minimum of 40 acres in a continuous unit, were classified into ecological types based on criteria established by the Fish and Wildlife Service and described in its Special Scientific Report: Wildlife No. 20, June 1953. These areas were then evaluated on a basis of their present usefulness to waterfowl. Similar treatment was given to a small number of open fresh water areas that fall within the limitations for Types 5 and 14, and to mud flats (Type 19) exposed at mean low tide.

1

In New Jersey, the inventory was made possible by cooperation of the following members of the State Division of Fish and Game: Director A. H. Underhill, who volunteered full cooperation of the entire Division; Superintendent of Game Management L. G. MacNamara who, in addition to delineating the regions containing wetlands of importance in the State, assisted in wetlands evaluations, provided information relative to land-use changes, wetlands development, and other wildlife uses, and offered many helpful suggestions in connection with the inventory; Biologists F. V. Schmidt, Fred Ferrigno, and Paul D. McLain, who evaluated most of the coastal marshes, provided information relative to other wildlife uses and development areas, and contributed many helpful suggestions. Officials of the State of New Jersey have concurred in the findings of this inventory.

U. S. Soil Conservation Service personnel who cooperated in the inventory are as follows: State Conservationist Frank C. Edminster provided a list of SCS employees in the State and offered their services; Work Unit Conservationists J. William Bellis, G. Sterling Otis, and Joseph J. Voschin provided aerial photographs, working space, and information relative to land capability classes.

2. Procedures. - Typing of wetlands areas was accomplished, with few exceptions, by field examination. The exceptions were Hackensack River, Crosswicks Creek, and a few interior areas. These were typed from aerial photographs, with the aid of field checks. Type 19 areas were determined through use of and measured on Coast and Geodetic Survey maps. Acreages of other types were obtained by planimetering

on U.S.G.S. maps or maps prepared by the New Jersey Department of Conservation and Economic Development. Occasionally, areas were encountered in which types were interspersed or for some other reason presented unusual problems in delineation. In such cases, type composition was estimated percentagewise. Categories available to State personnel for the evaluation of specific wetland areas were High, Moderate, Low, and Negligible.

Reliability of evaluation data is thought to be excellent, since State personnel were very familiar with conditions in virtually all included areas. Insofar as typing is concerned, however, considerable opportunity for error existed. Aerial photographs for the inland marshes and Hackensack River were old, dull, and usually too widely spaced for stereoscopic use. All these areas were visited but much of each of them was not readily accessible. An attempt was made to type coastal marshes by use of aerial photographs, but this technique was discarded as not feasible. Many of the marshes examined were broad and sometimes separated by broad expanses of water. Some were readily accessible at only a few points and some could be viewed only at a distance. Within the limits of time available for this work, closer examination was impossible. Interspersion of types and key plant species further complicated the situation. Percentagewise estimates of component types are thought to be reasonable, of course, but a time-consuming study would be necessary to prove or disprove their accuracy.

3. Coverage. -- Plate 2 (page A-17) shows the general areas which L. G. MacNamara delineated for inclusion in the wetland inventory. All of the tidal marshes of 40 acres or more in size and all mud flats within

3

the delineated regions were given complete coverage. Since very little tidal marsh occurs in single segments of less than 40 acres, coverage is believed to be very close to 100 percent.

In addition to the tidal wetlands, five inland regions were delineated as being important to waterfowl in New Jersey. Three of these were given complete coverage due to the contiguous nature of the wetlands included, with no small outlying segments. The Colliers Mills region, in the northeastern corner of Ocean County, is meant to include only the waters of nine artificial impoundments, and other wetland segments within the boundaries were not meant for inclusion in this inventory. One hundred percent of the water area of the impoundments has been included in this inventory. The fifth delineated inland region, that shown on Plate 2 between the Metedeconk and Navesink Rivers, is the only delineated region in the State where better than 99 percent coverage is estimated to have been accomplished and better than 95 percent coverage is estimated to have been accomplished there. This last region contains a very small fraction of the wetlands covered within the total of all delineated regions in New Jersey.

It is believed that over 99 percent coverage of the total wetlands within the delineated regions was accomplished in New Jersey. Data compiled by the Washington Office, River Basin Studies, indicate that 367,160 acres of wetlands occur in New Jersey, of which 240,230 acres are tidal marsh, 55,650 acres are inland marsh, and 71,280 acres are swamp. Comparison of the total mentioned above with applicable inventory totals derived from Table 1 shows some 111,780 acres of wetland in New Jersey not included within delineated retions. Further

4

Plate I

Physiographic Regions in New Jersey

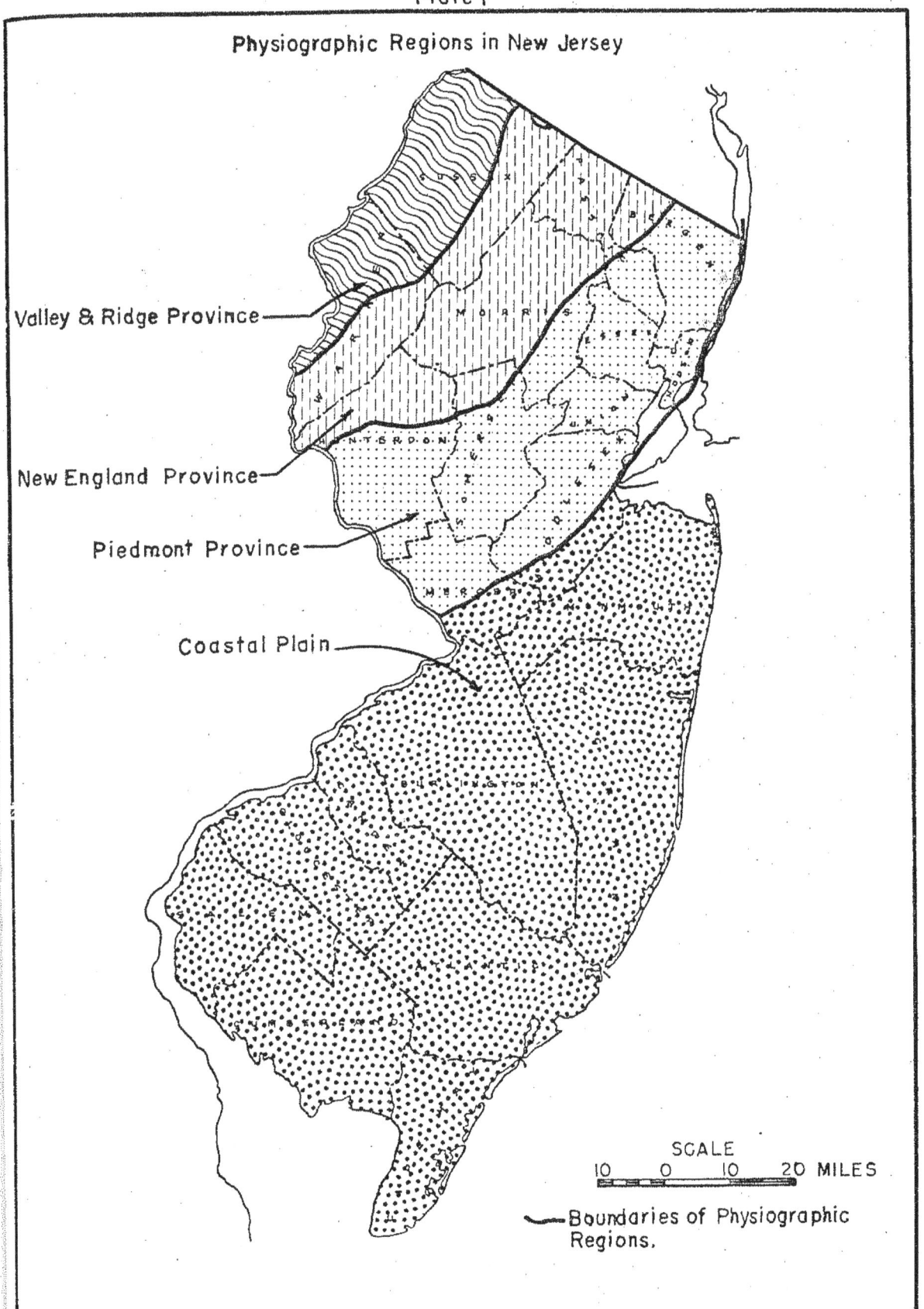

Valley & Ridge Province

New England Province

Piedmont Province

Coastal Plain

SCALE

10   0   10   20 MILES

Boundaries of Physiographic
Regions.

TABLE 1
STATE SUMMARY
WETLAND CLASSIFICATION AND EVALUATION

State   New Jersey

Wetland Category	Wetland Type*	Wetland Acreage by Waterfowl Value				Total Acreage by Types
		High	Moderate	Low	Negligible	
nland Fresh	2	10	40	1,280		1,330
"	3	2,090	920	290		3,300
"	4		20	30		50
"	5	140	40	190		370
"	6	260	70	620		950
"	7	2,070	880	5,580		8,530
"	8			160		160
oastal Fresh	12	29,760	8,330	17,770	850	56,710
"	13	12,110	920	10		13,040
"	14	80	240			320
astal Saline	16	58,850	86,070	5,520		150,440
"	18	10,300	10,390	180		20,870
"	19	11,790	1,220	770		13,780
State Totals		127,460	109,140	32,400	850	269,850

*List non-add items separately

Checked By _____   Approved By _____

Fish and Wildlife Service, Region __5__ Date __March 1954__

rior—Duplicating Section, Washington, D. C.

55434

comparison of Table 1 totals with Washington Office data shows approximately 50,000 acres of wetland not included in this inventory to be inland marsh, and the remaining 61,000 acres to be swamp.

4. _Description of Wetland Types Found in New Jersey._ - Wetland areas inventoried in New Jersey fall into three general categories containing a total of 13 specific types. Inland Fresh Areas include seven types, and Coastal Fresh Areas and Coastal Saline Areas three each. Following is a brief description of each specific type under the general category in which it occurs:

a. _Inland Fresh Areas_

Type 2 - _Fresh Meadows._ Soil waterlogged through most of the growing season. Vegetation of various grasses and sedges.

Type 3 - _Shallow Fresh Marshes - Inland._ Soil normally waterlogged during the growing season. May be flooded with as much as six inches of water at times. Vegetation grasses, cattails, and bulrushes.

Type 4 - _Deep Fresh Marshes - Inland._ Soil covered with from six inches to three feet of water during growing season. Emergent vegetation mainly cattails with round-stemmed bulrushes. Some true aquatics including pondweeds occur in small open areas of water.

Type 5 - _Open Fresh Water - Inland._ Open water up to 10 feet deep. Vegetation lacking in some of these units. Various annual seed plants and various grains including millet artificially maintained by management in Colliers Mills region.

7

Type 6 - Shrub Swamps. Soil normally waterlogged during the growing season and may be covered with as much as six inches of water at times. Vegetation of dogwood, alder, willow, and buttonbush.

Type 7 - Wooded Swamps. Soil normally waterlogged during the growing season. Vegetation varied but contains one or more of the following trees: red maple, oak, elm, swamp black gum, white cedar, and ash.

Type 8 - Bogs. Soil usually waterlogged; generally blanketed with a spongy covering of mosses or other plant material. Vegetation woody or herbaceous or both. Cranberries and leather-leaf are common in this State.

b. Coastal Fresh Areas

Type 12 - Shallow Fresh Marshes - Coastal. Soil always waterlogged during growing season and may be covered with as much as six inches of water at high tide. Main vegetative species are: phragmites (reed), big cordgrass, cattails, threesquares, and maidencane. Any one or combination of these species may be present in a specific wetland unit.

Type 13 - Deep Fresh Marshes - Coastal. Soil covered with from six inches to three feet of water at average high tide during growing season. Vegetation consists of cattails, wildrice, and bulrushes.

Type 14 - Open Fresh Water - Coastal. Water of variable depth, usually less than ten feet. When vegetation is present, it consists of true aquatics such as pondweeds.

c. Coastal Saline Areas

Type 16 - Salt Meadows. Soil always waterlogged during growing season. Rarely entirely covered with tidewater. Vegetation mainly saltmeadow cordgrass, saltgrass, and threesquares.

Type 18 - Salt Marshes. Soil covered at average high tide with six inches or more of water during the growing season. Main vegetative cover is saltmarsh cordgrass.

Type 19 - Sounds and Bays. For purposes of this inventory this type includes mud flats exposed at mean low tide. Vegetation usually scarce or lacking.

5. Waterfowl Values of Wetland Types by Physiographic Regions. Plate 1 (page 5) shows the locations of the four physiographic regions which occur in New Jersey. All the wetlands which have been delineated for inventory occur within two of these physiographic regions: the Piedmont Province and the Coastal Plain.

The Piedmont Province contains 20,110 acres, about 7.5 percent of the total wetland acreage inventoried in New Jersey, and is of relatively minor importance compared with the total wetland acreage inventoried in the State. The most important wetlands in this physiographic region are some 3,100 acres of High and Moderate value inland marsh (Types 2, 3, and 4) and 770 acres of High and Moderate value swamp located in Troy Meadows and Black Meadows in Morris County. These 3,000-odd acres represent all the inland marsh area of greater than Low value that was classified in the entire State. Of the remaining 17,010 acres of wetlands which were classified in the Piedmont Province, 12,210

9

acres are Low value, shallow, fresh coastal marsh (Type 12) occurring in the Hackensack Meadows, and over 4,000 acres are Low value inland fresh marsh and swamp located in Great Piece Meadows.

The Coastal Plain is the important physiographic region in New Jersey, containing 92.5 percent (249,740 acres) of all the wetland inventoried in the State. All of the coastal marshes and mud flats of High or Moderate waterfowl value in New Jersey, some 230,000 acres, are located within this physiographic region. With the exception of 9,670 acres of coastal marsh along the upper part of Barnegat Bay and the south shore of Raritan Bay, which are of Low value, only a few hundred acres of all coastal marsh in the southern half of New Jersey are of less than moderate importance to waterfowl. A great deal of wintering and migratory use is made of these marshes by black ducks and the coastal marshes and mud flats between the lower part of Barnegat Bay and the southern tip of Cape May provide one of the foremost wintering grounds for brant in the United States. Within this physiographic region, also, the salt meadows in the Egg Island region of Cumberland County are part of an important wintering area for snow geese. Pintails make heavy use of the fresh coastal marshes along streams tributary to Delaware Bay and the Delaware River during migration. Most of the remaining 9,000 acres of wetland not of the coastal marsh type which were inventoried in this physiographic region are wooded swamp, with small acreages of bog, shrub swamp and inland open fresh water.

6. Contribution of Wetland Types to Other Wildlife. - Table 2 indicates generally the kinds and extent of uses which wildlife species,

10

TABLE 2

GENERAL VALUES OF WETLAND TYPES TO OTHER WILDLIFE

SPECIES	2	3	4	5	6	7	8	12	13	14	16	18	19
Beaver	M-2bc	M-2bcd	M-2bcd	M-1a	H-1a	H-1a							
Clapper Rail								M-1bcd	M-1bcd		M-1bcd	H-1bcd	
Deer	M-2bcd				M-1a	M-1a		M-1cde					
Fox	M-2a	L-1cde			M-1a	M-1a					H-2a	H-2a	M-2a
Mink	M-1a	M-1a	M-1a	M-2a	L-1a	L-1a		M-1a	M-1a	M-2a	L-2a	L-1a	L-2a
Muskrat	M-1a	M-1a	M-1a	M-2a	L-1a	L-1a	L-1a	H-1a	H-1a	M-2a	M-1a	H-1a	M-2a
Otter	L-2a	L-1a	M-1a	H-2bcd	M-3a	M-3a	L-2bcd	L-1a	M-1a	H-2a	M-2a	M-2a	H-2a
Pheasant	M-1cde	M-3cde			M-3a	M-3a		M-3cde					
Raccoon	L-2bcd	M-1a	M-2bcd	L-2bcd	M-1a	M-1a	L-2bcd	M-1a	M-1a	L-2a	H-2a	M-2a	M-2a
Snipe	H-1bcd	M-1bcd						H-1bcd	M-1bcd				
Sora Rail	L-1bcd	L-1bcd	L-1bcd					H-1bcd	H-1bcd		L-1bcd	L-1bcd	
Woodcock					H-1bcd	H-1bcd							

Value Categories

H - High
M - Moderate
L - Low

Use Categories

1 - Food and Cover
2 - Food
3 - Cover

Time Categories

a - Year round   d - Fall
b - Spring   e - Winter
c - Summer

11

other than waterfowl, make of each wetland type inventoried in New Jersey. The three important species, other than waterfowl, most closely associated with the wetlands of New Jersey are muskrats, clapper rails, and sora rails. Muskrats provide an important source of income to many residents, especially in the southern part of the State. They occur in harvestable numbers in most of the coastal and inland marshes, with especially large populations in the various coastal fresh marshes (Types 12 and 13). Clapper rails are an important game bird in the coastal marshes between lower Barnegat Bay and Cape May on the ocean side of New Jersey. One of the most important game birds of the Delaware Bay side of southern New Jersey is the sora rail. Especially high concentrations of this species occur in the fresh coastal marshes along streams tributary to Delaware Bay and the Delaware River. The tidal fresh marshes along the Maurice River in Cumberland County provide one of the most popular sora-rail hunting areas in New Jersey.

7. <u>Land-Use Changes Affecting Wetlands</u>. - Present trends indicate that the greatest threat to New Jersey wetlands lies in the practice of filling such areas to create sites for housing and industrial development and highways. Pollution is also a factor which must be considered. It may not actually destroy wetlands but it may destroy or seriously reduce their usefulness as wildlife habitat. Although not at present properly classified as a land-use trend, extensive ditching of wetlands in the past in an effort to control mosquito populations has resulted in tremendous loss of value in wildlife wetland habitat. While some of that habitat has been improving due to the gradually decreasing effectiveness

12

of unmaintained ditches, many miles of ditches are currently being rejuvenated, with a resulting loss of value of the affected wetlands to wildlife.

The threatening land-use trends listed above are not necessarily associated with the Soil Conservation Service's land capability classes. Location seems to be the primary consideration. Lands in the vicinity of growing settlements or near areas that may be developed for recreational purposes are particularly vulnerable. As much as $5,000 per acre is being paid for good farmland for development in such areas. Wetlands usually would sell for much less than that figure and, consequently, would be much more in demand where available.

From a wildlife standpoint, it would perhaps seem logical to concentrate on preservation of wetlands that are most important to wildlife, and development of those that with least effort can provide the greatest benefit to wildlife. Further examination might suggest, however, that the cause would be furthered by acquisition first of those wetlands that are in most danger of being lost, the expectation being that those less favorably located for housing and industrial development would be reasonably safe for the immediate future without further protection. In suitable areas that are in locations in which intensive mosquito control is desirable, mosquito control through water level control in conjunction with development of wetlands for wildlife could well result in the realization of both objectives with mutual advantages.

8. _Improvement of Wetlands for Wildlife_. -- Development of wetlands in the interest of wildlife, particularly waterfowl, was begun by the Division of Fish and Game about 15 years ago. That effort

13

involved a dike with water control structure which converted a salt-marsh into an area of controllable water depth capable of supporting the growth of fresh-water plants.   So successful was the project that others of a similar nature were soon to follow.   Intensive research has been and is being carried on, in connection with these developments, in an attempt to determine, among other things, the most effective systems of water-level manipulations for promoting the growth of species of plants desired for any particular purpose.   Although much remains to be learned, results of that research have been so favorable that new developments may now be brought into high production within a period shorter by several years than was being realized prior to the time this new knowledge became available.   Much has been learned also about the effects of water-level fluctuations upon each of several species of mosquitoes.

Inland wetland areas were developed later through the use of low earth-fill dams with water control structures.   One of the most productive techniques utilized in connection with this sort of project was that of tilling and fertilizing the soil during drawdown, and planting seed-bearing crops to be inundated for the use of waterfowl.

These projects have met with tremendous success as measured by increase in rate of duck use.   Opening potholes in salt marshes by means of dynamite or mechanical means is another technique that has been successful in increasing duck use.

Expansion of this program for wetland development by the Division of Fish and Game is not only recommended but urged.   Similar

14

type projects on a smaller scale could be undertaken by local groups such as sporting clubs and the like. Small pond development and series of ponds with controllable water levels are adaptable to such sponsorship and if widely promoted could contribute much to wetlands wildlife. Private owners of saltmarshes frequently are interested in increasing production of fur animals on their holdings. In many cases that could be accomplished by freshening the marshes through the use of dikes, and the result would also be an improvement for waterfowl.

Since highways frequently destroy wetlands or seriously reduce their value, it would seem desirable and appropriate that officials of the agencies involved arrange to have a biologist attached to the Division of Highways for the purpose of examining new road plans for possible sites that are adaptable for wetland development in conjunction with highway construction. The "thousand-acre marsh" near Delaware City, Delaware, is an outstanding example of a valuable wetland development simply and economically achieved by constructing a water control structure in a culvert under a highway embankment.

9. Summary. - Over 90 percent of the important wetlands for waterfowl in New Jersey occur within the Coastal Plain region of the southern half of the State. The tidal marshes in this physiographic region receive heavy waterfowl utilization during migration and support considerable numbers of wintering ducks, brant, and geese. In addition to waterfowl importance, these same tidal marshes produce fair to excellent muskrat habitat and also support clapper and sora rails in sufficient numbers to provide good hunting. The most serious threats

15

to New Jersey wetlands are: filling, mosquito-control ditching, and pollution. Filling for reasons of industrial expansion, highway construction, and summer-home development presents the greatest hazard. Selection of the most expedient methods of wetlands preservation and development presents a formidable problem. It might seem logical to concentrate effort on preserving the most important and developing that which returns most for the money. On the other hand, further investigation might suggest that greater over-all benefit would be realized through acquisition first of those wetlands in most danger of being lost. The New Jersey Division of Fish and Game has done and is doing considerable marsh development work, especially on coastal marshes, in the interest of waterfowl and muskrats. Continuation and expansion of this program should help to offset losses through filling, and also may replace some mosquito-control ditching with water-level manipulations which would be mutually advantageous for wildlife and mosquito-control purposes.

COUNTY SUMMARY

WETLAND CLASSIFICATION AND EVALUATION

County __Atlantic__

State __New Jersey__

No. of Wetland Units: Specific __8__

Generalized __--__

Wetland Type*	Frequency of Occurrence	Commonly Associated Types	Wetland Acreage by Waterfowl Value					Use By Waterfowl**	Land Capability Class(es)	Dominant Natural Plants or Agricultural Use
			High	Mod.	Low	Negl.	Total			
7	9	12	1,230				1,230	D-1	8	Red maple, elm, oak, cedar
12	14	16,13	4,130	450		40	4,620	D-4,3,2	8	Big cordgrass, threesquares, phragmites (reed) and cattails
13	3	12,16	720				720	D-2,4,3	8	Cattails, bulrushes
16	--	18,12	28,950	8,560			37,510	D-4,3,2 Brant-4,2	8	Saltmeadow cordgrass, salt-grass, and threesquares.
18	--	16,19	4,190	380			4,570	D-4,3 Brant-4	8	Saltmarsh cordgrass
19	35	18,16	3,390	190			3,580	D-2,4,3 Brant-2,4,4	--	--
County Totals			42,610	9,580		40	52,230			

*List non-add items separately
**Indicate by letter and number in order of importance:
D-Ducks; G-Geese; B-Geese and 1-... ; 2-Feeding;
3-Migrating; 4-Wintering

Fish and Wildlife Service, Region __5__

By _____ Date __March 1964__

No. of Wetland Units: Specific 1

Generalized ___

County Bergen

State New Jersey

Wet-land Type*	Frequency of Occurrence	Commonly Associated Types	Wetland Acreage by Waterfowl Value						Use By Waterfowl**	Land Capability Class(es)	Dominant Natural Plants or Agricultural Use
			High	Mod.	Low	Negl.	Total				
12	--	--			6,310		6,310	D-2,3,4	8	Threesquares and cattails, phragmites (reeds), big cordgrass
County Totals					6,310		6,310			

*List non-add items separately
**Indicate by letter and number in order of importance:
D-Ducks; G-Geese; C-Coots; and 1-Breeding; 2-Feeding;
3-Migrating; 4-Wintering

Interior—Duplicating Section, Washington, D. C.

Fish and Wildlife Service, Region 5

By _____ Date March 1954

55-436

No. of Wetland Units: Specific 6

Generalized ____

County Burlington

State New Jersey

Wetland Type*	Frequency of Occurrence	Commonly Associated Types	Wetland Acreage by Waterfowl Value					Use By Waterfowl**	Land Capability Class(es)	Dominant Natural Plants or Agricultural Use
			High	Mod.	Low	Negl.	Total			
6	1	7,12	10				10	D-1	8	Dogwood, alder
7	1	6,12,13	50				50	D-1	8	Red maple, elm, oak, black gum.
12	18	6,7,13,16	5,050				5,050	D-4,3,2,1	8	Big cordgrass, phragmites(reed cattails and threesquares
13	16	12,7	1,940				1,940	D-4,3,2,1	8	Cattails,wildrice,bulrushes.
16	--	12,18	2,880				2,880	D-2,4,3	8	Saltmeadow cordgrass, salt-grass and threesquares
18	--	16	60				60	D-4,3,2	8	Saltmarsh cordgrass
19	3	--	130				130	D-2	--	--
County Totals			10,120				10,120			

A-3

*List non-add items separately

**Indicate by letter and number in order of importance:
D-Ducks; G-Geese; C-Coots; and 1-Nesting; 2-Feeding; 3-Migrating; 4-Wintering

Interior—Duplicating Section, Washington, D. C.

Fish and Wildlife Service, Region 5

By _____ Date March 1954

55436

No. of Wetland Units: Specific __3__

                Generalized __=__

County __Camden__

State __New Jersey__

Wet- land Type*	Frequency of Occurrence	Commonly Associated Types	Wetland Acreage by Waterfowl Value					Use By Waterfowl**	Land Capability Class(es)	Dominant Natural Plants or Agricultural Use
			High	Mod.	Low	Negl.	Total			
12	5	13,19	480				480	D-4,2,3	8	Phragmites(reed),cattails
13	5	12,19	910				910	D-4,2,3	8	Cattails, bulrushes
19	3	13,12	360				360	D-2,3,4	1	--
County Totals			1,750				1,750			

*List non-add items separately
**Indicate by letter and number in order of importance:
   D-Ducks; G-Geese; C-Coots; and 1-Nesting; 2-Feeding;
   3-Migrating; 4-Wintering

Interior—Duplicating Section, Washington, D. C.

Fish and Wildlife Service, Region __5__

By_____ Date __March 1954__

55436

No. of Wetland Units: Specific 16

Generalized ""

County Cape May

State New Jersey

Wet-land Type*	Frequency of Occurrence	Commonly Associated Types	Wetland Acreage by Waterfowl Value					Use By Waterfowl**	Land Capability Class(es)	Dominant Natural Plants or Agricultural Use
			High	Mod.	Low	Negl.	Total			
7	3	12,18,16		230			230	D-1	8	Red maple, cedar, gum
12	24	16,18,13,7	110	1,570	540	470	2,690	D-1,2,3,4	8	Threesquares, big cordgrass, cattails, maidencane, and phragmites (reed).
13	3	12	290				290	D-2,3,1,4	8	Cattails, wildrice, bulrushes.
16	:	18,12	5,430	31,440	280		37,150	G-2 Brant-4 D-2,4	8	Saltmeadow cordgrass, salt-grass and threesquares
18	:	16,12	470	7,770	10		8,250	Brant-4 D-4,1,3	8	Saltmarsh cordgrass
19	47	18,16,12	2,930	800	440		4,170	Brant-2,4 D-2,4,3	:	:
County Totals			9,230	41,810	1,270	470	52,780			

A-5

*List non-add items separately

**Indicate by letter and number in order of importance:
D-Ducks; G-Geese; C-Coots; and 1-Nesting; 2-Feeding; 3-Migrating; 4-Wintering;

Fish and Wildlife Service, Region 5

By _____ Date March 1954

Interior--Duplicating Section, Washington, D. C.

55-436

No. of Wetland Units: Specific 11

Generalized —

County Cumberland

State New Jersey

Wet-land Type*	Frequency of Occurrence	Commonly Associated Types	Wetland Acreage by Waterfowl Value					Use By Waterfowl**	Land Capability Class(es)	Dominant Natural Plants or Agricultural Use
			High	Mod.	Low	Negl.	Total			
7	3	12,18,16		80			80	D-1	8	Red maple, cedar, gum
12	22	16,13,14,18	1,670	5,170		300	7,140	D-1,2,3,4	8	Threesquares; big cordgrass, cattails, maidencane, and phragmites (reed).
13	14	12,14	1,520	900			2,420	D-2,3,1,4	8	Cattails, wildrice
14	2	13		240			240	D-2,3	8	Pondweeds
16	1	18,12	16,260	18,010			34,270	D-2,4 G-2,4	8	Saltmeadow cordgrass, salt-grass and threesquares.
18	1	16,12,7	4,500	1,100			5,600	D-4,1,3	8	Saltmarsh cordgrass
19	10	18,16,12	1,760	200			1,960	D-2	—	—
County Totals			25,710	25,700		300	51,710			

A-6

*List non-add items separately
**Indicate by letter and number in order of importance:
D-Ducks; G-Geese; C-Coots; and 1-Nesting; 2-Feeding;
3-Migrating; 4-Wintering

Fish and Wildlife Service, Region 5

By ——— Date March 1954

Interior--Duplicating Section, Washington, D. C.

55436

Form RBS-4
Rev. 8/53

COUNTY SUMMARY

WETLAND CLASSIFICATION AND EVALUATION

File No.

No. of Wetland Units: Specific 1

Generalized ...

County Essex

State New Jersey

Wet-land Type*	Frequency of Occurrence	Commonly Associated Types	Wetland Acreage by Waterfowl Value					Use By Waterfowl**	Land Capability Class(es)	Dominant Natural Plants or Agricultural Use
			High	Mod.	Low	Negl.	Total			
2	16	6,7,3			710		710	D-3,2	8	Grasses, sedges
3	5	2,7,4			230		230	D-3,2	8	Grasses, cattails, bulrushes
4	1	3,6,7			10		10	D-3,2	8	Cattails, pondweeds
6	8	2,7			330		330	D-3,1	8	Dogwood, alder, buttonbush, willow
7	13	6,2			1,460		1,460	D-1	8	Red maple, elm, ash
County Totals					2,740		2,740			

A-7

*List non-add items separately
**Indicate by letter and number in order of importance:
D-Ducks; G-Geese; C-Coots; and L-... ; 2-Feeding;
3-Migrating; 4-Wintering.

Fish and Wildlife Service, Region 5

By_____ Date March 1954

No. of Wetland Units: Specific ___4___

County ___Gloucester___

State ___New Jersey___

Generalized ___"___

Wet-land Type*	Frequency of Occurrence	Commonly Associated Types	Wetland Acreage by Waterfowl Value					Use By Waterfowl**	Land Capability Class(es)	Dominant Natural Plants or Agricultural Use
			High	Mod.	Low	Negl.	Total			
12	9	13,19	1,320				1,320	D-2,1,4,3	8	Threesquares, phragmites(reed) cattail and big cordgrass
13	7	12,19	2,030				2,030	D-2,1,4,3	8	Cattails,wildrice,bulrushes
19	11	13,12	870				870	D-2,3,4	-	--
County Totals			4,220				4,220			

A-8

*List non-add items separately
**Indicate by letter and number in ___ of importance:
D-Ducks; G-Geese; C-Coots; and 1-___; 2-Feeding;
3-Migrating; 4-Wintering

Interior--Duplicating Section, Washington, D. C.

Fish and Wildlife Service, Region __5__

By _____ Date March 1954

55436

COUNTY SUMMARY

WETLAND CLASSIFICATION AND EVALUATION

File No. _____

No. of Wetland Units: Specific __1__

Generalized ____

County __Hudson__

State __New Jersey__

Wetland Type*	Frequency of Occurrence	Commonly Associated Types	Wetland Acreage by Waterfowl Value					Use By Waterfowl**	Land Capability (Classes)	Dominant Natural Plants or Agricultural Use
			High	Mod.	Low	Negl.	Total			
12	1				5,900		5,900	D-2,3,4	8	Phragmites (reed), big cordgrass, cattails, and threesquares.
County Totals					5,900		5,900			

*List non-add items separately
**Indicate by letter and number in order of importance:
D-Ducks; G-Geese; C-Coots and ...; 2-Feeding;
3-Migrating; 4-Wintering

Fish and Wildlife Service, Region __5__

By_____ Date __March 1954__

A-9

Interior-Duplicating Section, Washington, D. C.

No. of Wetland Units: Specific 2

Generalized ___

County Middlesex

State New Jersey

Wetland Type*	Frequency of Occurrence	Commonly Associated Types	Wetland Acreage by Waterfowl Value					Use By Waterfowl**	Land Capability Class(es)	Dominant Natural Plants or Agricultural Use
			High	Mod.	Low	Negl.	Total			
12	6	16			510		510	D-4,3,2,1	8	Big cordgrass, phragmites (reed) and threesquares.
16	-	12,18			860		860	D-4	8	Saltmeadow cordgrass, saltgrass and threesquares
18	-	16			20		20	D-4	8	Saltmarsh cordgrass
County Totals					1,390		1,390			

*List non-agricultural items separately
**Indicate by letter and number in order of importance:
    D-Ducks; G-Geese, Swans and Brant; 2-Feeding;
    3-Migrating; 4-Wintering;

Interior-Duplicating Section, Washington, D. C.

Fish and Wildlife Service, Region 5

By ___ Date March 1954

A - 11

36436

No. of Wetland Units: Specific 13

Generalized -

County Monmouth

State New Jersey

Wet-land Type*	Frequency of Occurrence	Commonly Associated Types	Wetland Acreage by Waterfowl Value					Use By Waterfowl**	Land Capability Class(es)	Dominant Natural Plants or Agricultural Use
			High	Mod.	Low	Negl.	Total			
6	1	7			40		40	D-1	8	Willow, alder, dogwood
7	24	12,8,6			2,360		2,360	D-1	8	Red maple, elm, cedar
8	3	7			160		160	D-2	8	Cranberries, leatherleaf
12	16	16,13,7			1,470		1,470	D-1,4,3	8	Phragmites(reed), big cord-grass and threesquares
13	2	12			10		10	D-2,4,3	8	Cattails, bulrushes
16	-	12,18			730		730	D-4,3	8	Saltmeadow cordgrass, salt-grass and threesquares
18	-	16			30		30	D-4,3	8	Saltmarsh, cordgrass
19	13	-	80		330		410	D-2	-	--
County Totals			80		5,130		5,210			

A-12

*List non-ag items separately

**Indicate by letter and number in order of importance:
D-Ducks; G-Geese, A-... and ...; 2-Feeding;
3-Migrating; 4-Wintering

Fish and Wildlife Service, Region 5

By _____ Date March 1954

No. of Wetland Units: Specific 5

Generalized

County Morris

State New Jersey

Wetland Type*	Frequency of Occurrence	Commonly Associated Types	Wetland Acreage by Waterfowl Value					Use By Waterfowl**	Land Capability Class(es)	Dominant Natural Plants or Agricultural Use
			High	Mod.	Low	Negl.	Total			
2	19	3,6,7	10	40	570		620	D-3,2,1	8	Grasses, sedges
3	16	2,6,7,4	2,090	920	60		3,070	D-3,2,1	8	Cattails, grasses, bulrushes
4	4	3,7	20	20	20		40	D-3,2,1	8	Cattails, pondweeds
6	24	7,2,3	220	70	250		540	D-1	8	Alder, dogwood, buttonbush, willow
7	41	6,2,3	320	160	410		890	D-1	8	Red maple, elm, ash
County Totals			2,640	1,210	1,310		5,160			

A-13

*List non-add items separately

**Indicate by letter and number all types of importance:

D-Ducks; G-Geese; ... and ... 1-Breeding; 2-Feeding;

3-Migrating; 4-Wintering

Fish and Wildlife Service, Region 5

By_____ Date March 1954

Interior-Duplicating Section, Washington, D. C.

No. of Wetland Units: Specific __11__

Generalized __--__

County __Ocean__

State __New Jersey__

Wetland Type*	Frequency of Occurrence	Commonly Associated Types	Wetland Acreage by Waterfowl Value					Use By Waterfowl**	Land Capability Class(es)	Dominant Natural Plants or Agricultural Use
			High	Mod.	Low	Negl.	Total			
5	10	7	140	40	190		370	D=2,3	8	--
7	10	12,16		410	1,350		1,760	D=1	8	Red maple, elm, cedar
12	35	16,7,9,13		1,140	2,270	40	3,450	D=2,3,4,1	8	Phragmites(reed), big cord-grass, cattails,threesquares
13	1	12		20			20	D-2,3,4	8	Cattails, pondweeds
16	--	12,18		28,060	3,650		31,710	Brant-4 / D-2,3,4	8	Saltmeadow, cordgrass, saltgrass, threesquares
18	--	16		1,140	120		1,260	Brant-2,4 / D-4,3	8	Saltmarsh, cordgrass
19	16	--	1,770	30			1,800	Brant-2,4 / D-2,4	-	--
County Totals			1,910	30,840	7,580	40	40,370			

A-14

*List non-add items separately

**Indicate by letter and number in order of importance:
D-Ducks; G-Geese; C-Coots; and 1-Nesting; 2-Feeding; 3-Migrating; 4-Wintering;

Interior—Duplicating Section, Washington, D. C.

Fish and Wildlife Service, Region 5

By _____ Date __March 1954__

No. of Wetland Units: Specific __6__   County __Salem__

State __New Jersey__

Generalized __–__

Wet-land Type*	Frequency of Occurrence	Commonly Associated Types	Wetland Acreage by Waterfowl Value					Use By Waterfowl**	Land Capability Class(es)	Dominant Natural Plants or Agricultural Use
			High	Mod.	Low	Negl.	Total			
7	1	12	190				190	D-1	8	Red maple, cedar
12	32	13,16,14	16,740		770		17,510	D-2,3,1,4	8	Big cordgrass, phragmites(reed cattails, threesquares
13	12	12	4,670				4,670	D-2,3,1,4	8	Cattails, wildrice
14	2	12	70				70	D-2,3,4	8	--
16	-	12,18	5,330				5,330	D-2,4	8	Saltmeadow, cordgrass,salt-grass, and threesquares
18	-	16,19	1,080				1,080	D-4,1,3	8	Saltmarsh cordgrass
19	4	18,16,12,13	500				500	D-2,3	-	--
County Totals			28,580		770		29,350			

A-15

*List non-aid items separately
**Indicate by letter and number in order of importance:
D-Ducks; G-Geese, etc.; and 1-Nesting; 2-Feeding;
3-Migrating; 4-Wintering

Interior--Duplicating Section, Washington, D. C.

Fish and Wildlife Service, Region __5__

By _____   Date __March 1954__

35435

COMMON AND SCIENTIFIC NAMES OF PLANTS MENTIONED

Alders, _Alnus_

Big cordgrass, _Spartina cynosuroides_

Black ash, _Fraxinus nigra_

Bulrushes, _Scirpus_

Buttonbush, _Cephalanthus occidentalis_

Carex, _Carex_

Cattails, _Typha_

Cranberries, _Vaccinium_

Dogwoods, _Cornus_

Eelgrass, _Zostera marina_

Elm, _Ulmus americana_

Glassworts, _Salicornia_

Grasses, _Gramineae_

Leather-leaf, _Chamaedaphne calyculata_

Maidencane, _Panicum hemitomon_

Overcup oak, _Quercus lyrata_

Pondweeds, _Potamogeton_

Red maple, _Acer rubrum_

Reed, _Phragmites communis_

Saltgrass, _Distichlis_

Saltmarsh cordgrass, _Spartina alterniflora_

Saltmeadow cordgrass, _Spartina patens_

Sedges, _Cyperaceae_

Swamp black gum, _Nyssa biflora_

Threesquares, _Scirpus americanus and olneyi_

Water oak, _Quercus nigra_

White cedar, _Thuja occidentalis_

Wild millet, _Echinochloa crusgalli_

Wildrice, _Zizania aquatica_

Willows, _Salix_

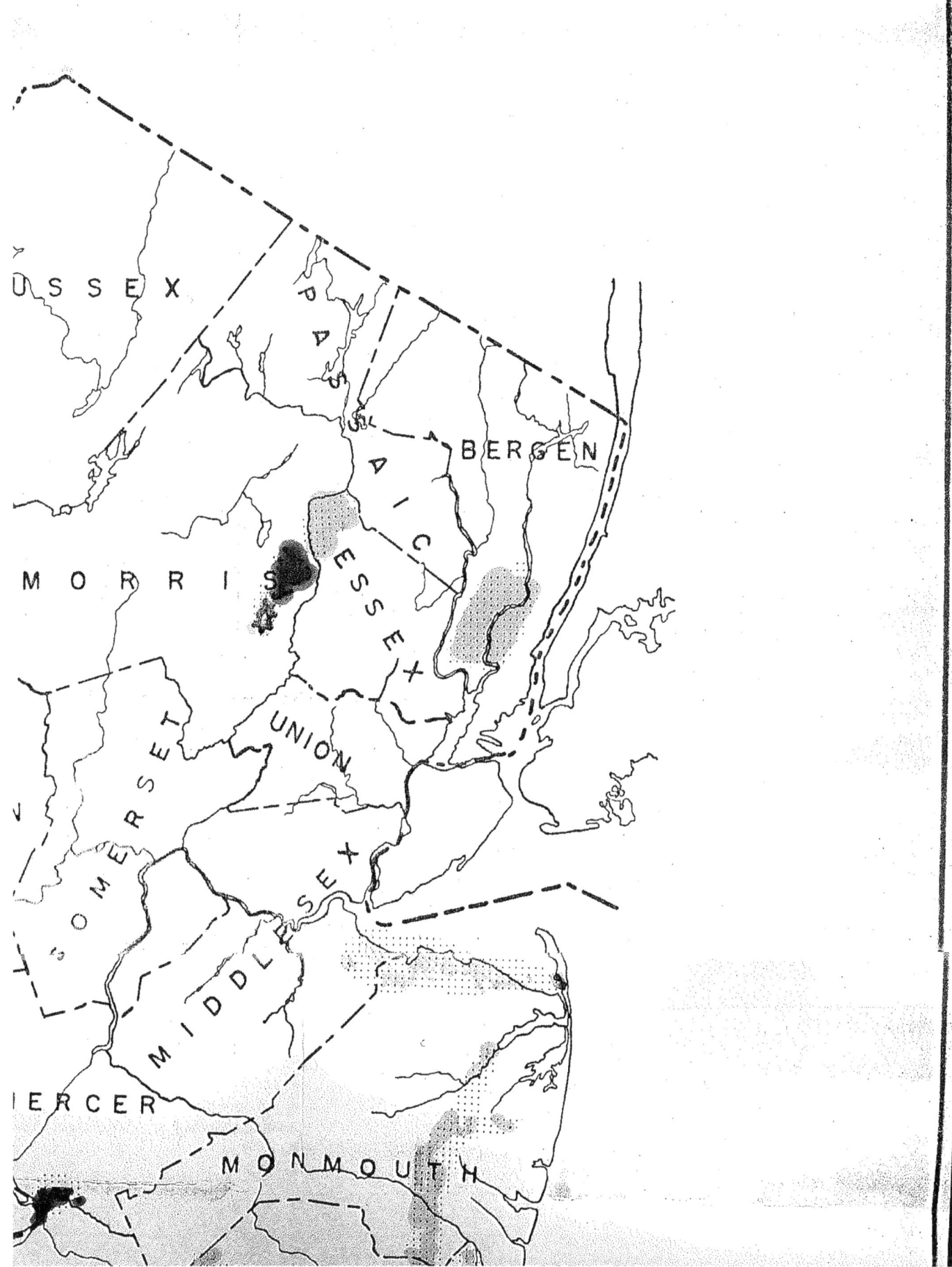

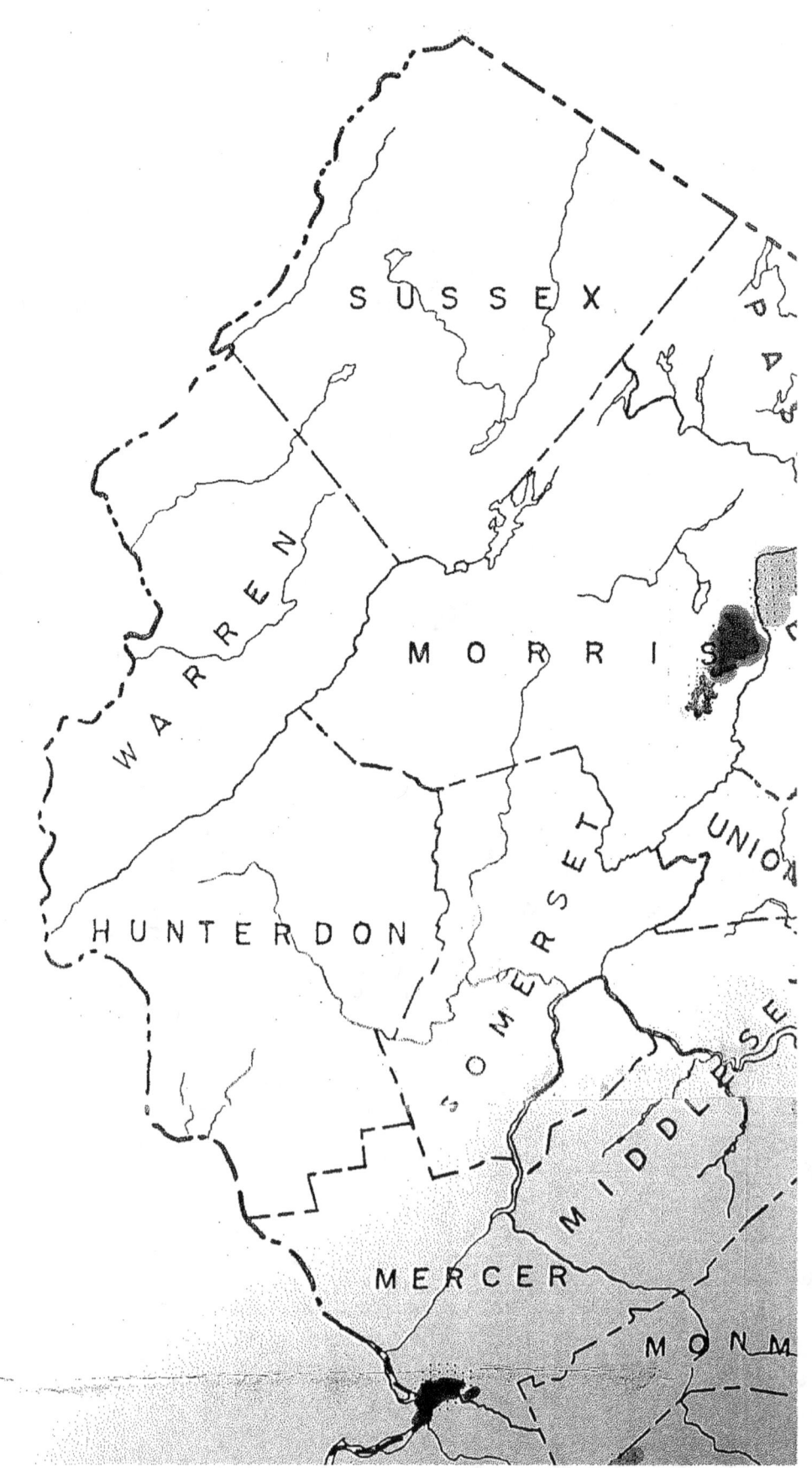

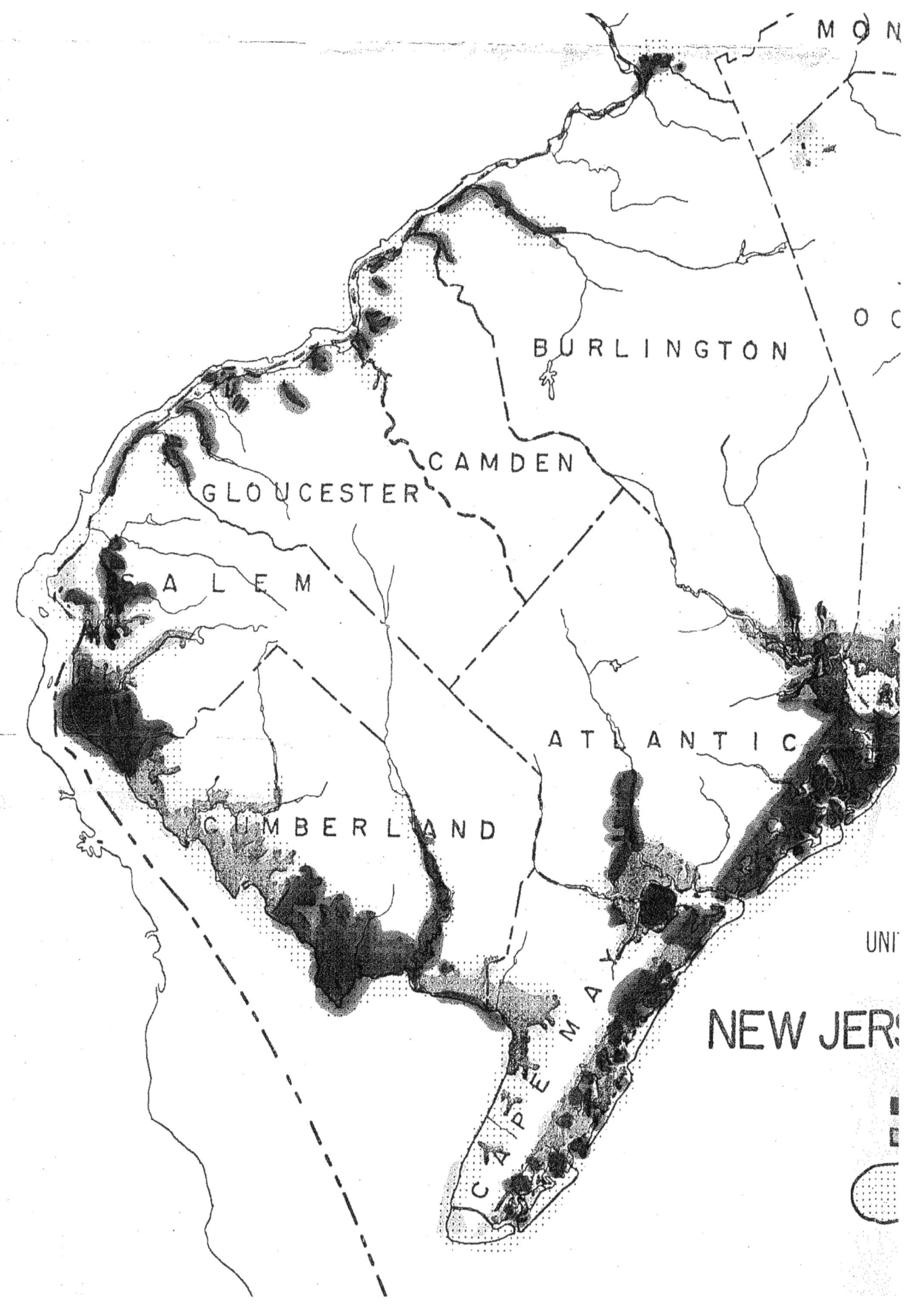

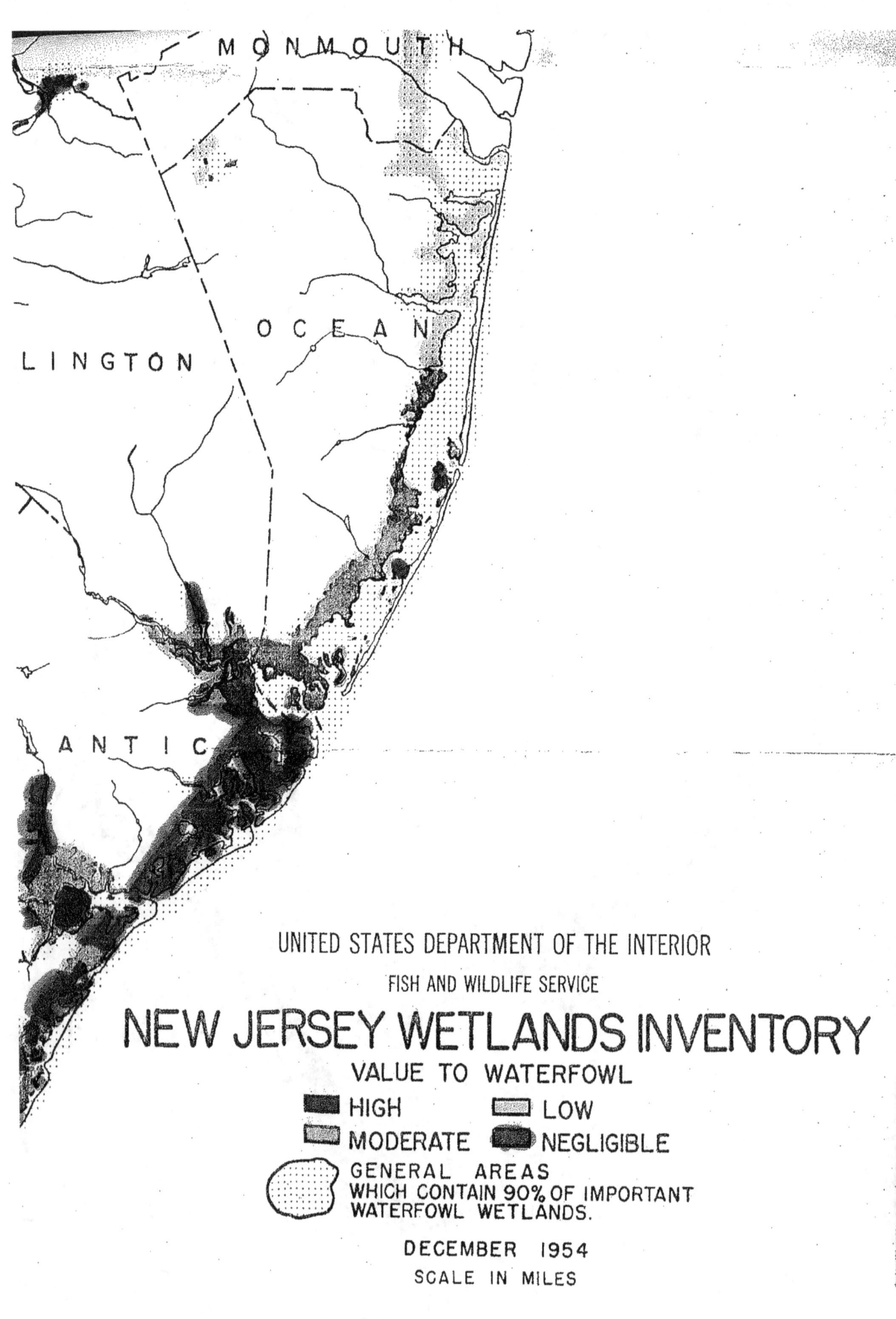

UNITED STATES DEPARTMENT OF THE INTERIOR

FISH AND WILDLIFE SERVICE

NEW JERSEY WETLANDS INVENTORY

VALUE TO WATERFOWL

- HIGH
- LOW
- MODERATE
- NEGLIGIBLE

GENERAL AREAS WHICH CONTAIN 90% OF IMPORTANT WATERFOWL WETLANDS.

DECEMBER 1954

SCALE IN MILES

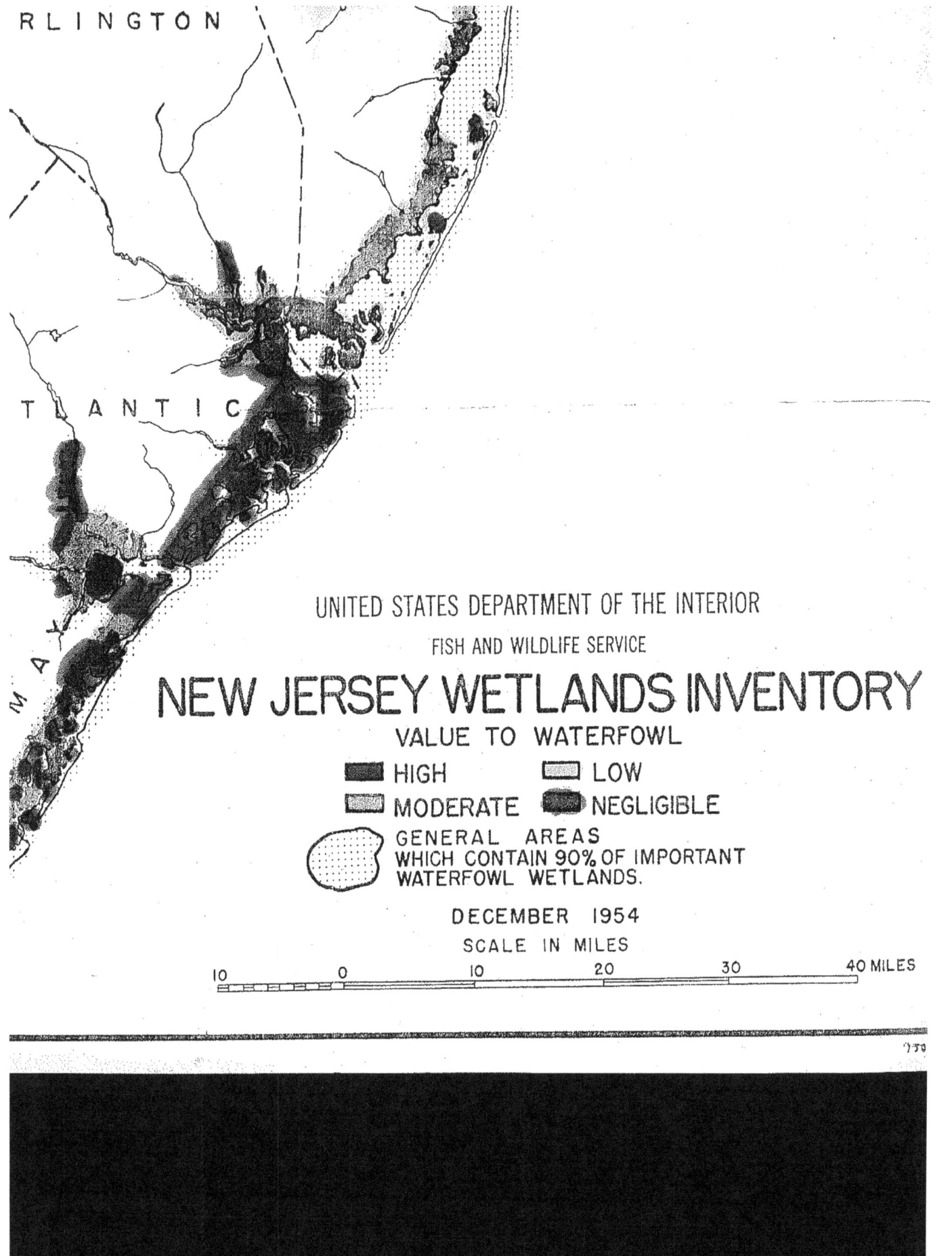

UNITED STATES DEPARTMENT OF THE INTERIOR

FISH AND WILDLIFE SERVICE

NEW JERSEY WETLANDS INVENTORY

VALUE TO WATERFOWL

HIGH   LOW

MODERATE   NEGLIGIBLE

GENERAL   AREAS
WHICH CONTAIN 90% OF IMPORTANT
WATERFOWL WETLANDS.

DECEMBER 1954

SCALE IN MILES

10   0   10   20   30   40 MILES

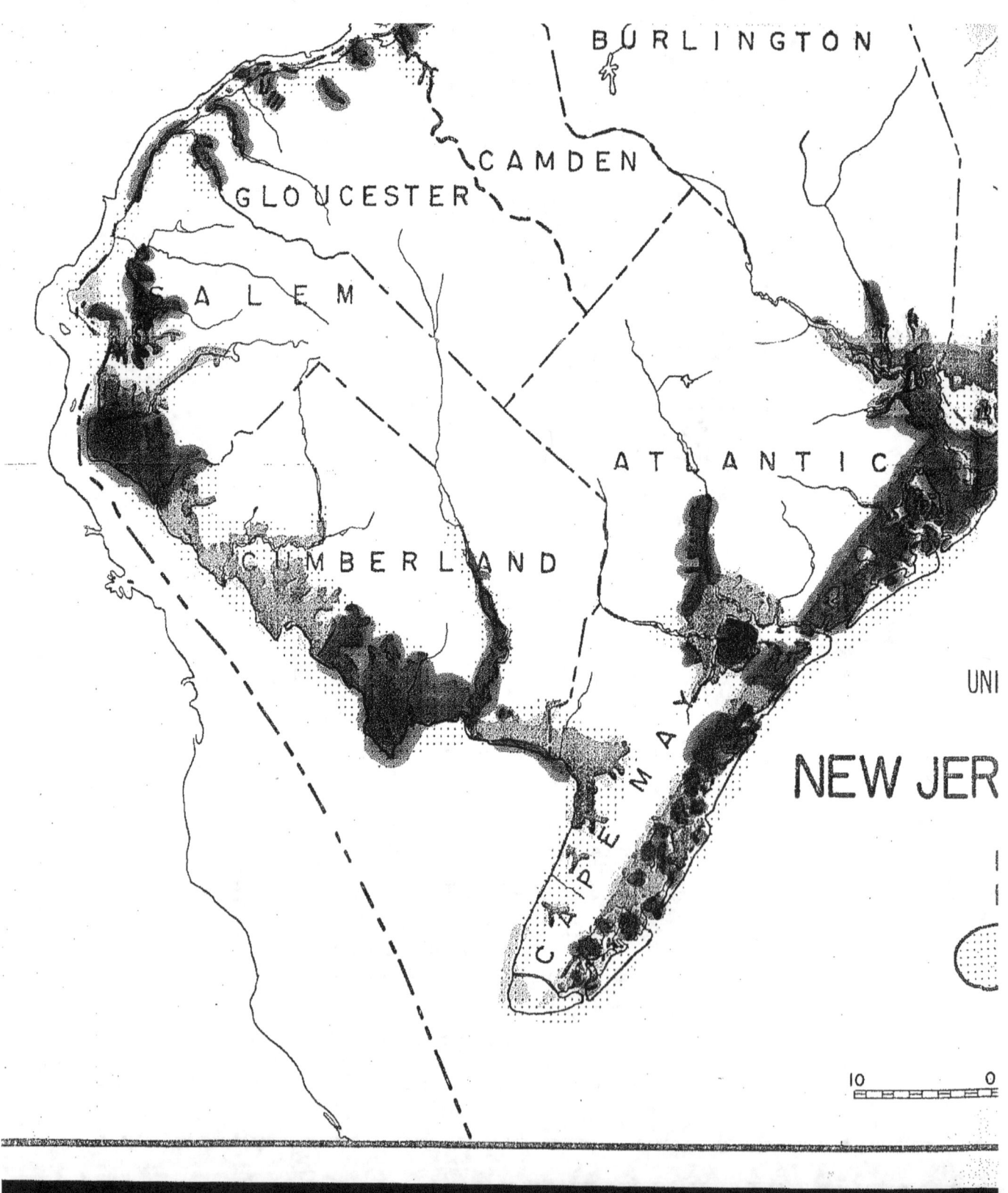